A Closer Look on Forensic Science

Archana Singh
LL.B., M.Sc. (Forensic Science)

Copyright © 2020 Archana Singh
All rights reserved.
ISBN: 9781691713189

A Closer Look on Forensic Science

First Edition: 2019

© Publisher

No part of this e-book may be reproduced or transmitted in any form or by any mean, mechanical or electronic form including recording or photocopying or by any other platform of information storage and retrieval system without permission from publisher of this e-book. If any part of this e-book or whole e-book will be found online on any platform without consent of author and publisher, then it will be decided only in court and compensation will be taken.

ISBN: 9781691713189

Price: 573/-

US$: $8

Disclaimer

Forensic science field is constantly changing. New research and experiences widen the scope, knowledge and information of forensic science. The Author and the editor have tried their best in providing information available to them at the time of book preparation. Although every efforts and care have been made to ensure the optimum accuracy of the information, yet it may be possible some errors might have been left uncorrected. The publisher, the printer, the author and the editor will not be held responsible for any inadvertent errors or inaccuracies.

Description

The "A Closer Look on Forensic Science" is the resource to provide comprehensive coverage on Forensic Science. This book will help you to gain knowledge about every aspect of Forensic Science, such as; History, Branches, Work, Organization, Crime Scene Investigation, Modus Operandi Bureau, Evidences, etc. This book is going to present an overview of Forensic Science so you will know what is it, why is it, what is the use of it, what is the limitations and much more. This e-book has contains basic knowledge of Forensic Science. Every word that confused you before is going to be solved after reading it.

Edited By *@forensicfield*

https://forensicfield.blog/

https://forensicfield.blogspot.com/

https://www.youtube.com/c/ForensicField/

https://www.facebook.com/forensicfield/

https://twitter.com/ForensicField

https://www.instagram.com/forensicfield/

https://www.linkedin.com/in/forensicfield/

INDEX

Chapter 1
Introduction

What is Forensic Science?	2
Is Criminalistics and Forensic Same?	2
What is Criminology?	2
Main Ingredients of Forensic Science	3
History of Forensic Science	5
Future of Forensic Science	12
Scope of Forensic Science	13
Need of Forensic Science	15
What is use of Forensic Science?	17
How Reliable Is Forensic Science?	17
Reel Vs. Reality	18

Chapter 2

Law and Forensic Science in India	20

Chapter 3
Eligibility

What Skills Are Involved In Forensic Science?	26
Eligibility for Forensic Science Courses	27

Chapter 4
Forensic Scientist

Work of Forensic Scientist	30
What Forensic Scientist Don't Do?	30
Responsibilities	31
What to expect?	32

Chapter 5

Tools & Techniques of Forensic Science	34

Chapter 6

Branches of Forensic Science   39

Chapter 7

Laws And Principles Of Forensic Science   45

Chapter 8

Investigation of the Crime Scene

What is crime scene?	49
Crime Scene Investigation	49
Investigation team of crime–scene	49
How is it possible to identify the person who committed a crime?	50
Who is a crime scene investigator?	51
Purpose of investigation	51
Types of crime scene	52
Identifying, establishing, protecting, and securing the boundaries	54
Documenting the scene and evidence	57
Responsibilities of lead investigator	64
Systematically search for evidence	65

Chapter 9

Modus Operandi

What is Modus Operandi?	69
Why Modus Operandi Is Used?	69
What Is Modus Operandi Bureau?	69
Types Of Modus Operandi	69
History Of Modus Operandi	69
How Modus Operandi Bureau Solves Crime?	71

Functions of Modus Operandi Bureau · 71

Chapter 10
Evidences

What is Evidence? · 74
Forensic Evidence · 74
Categories of Evidence · 74
Collection and Preservation of Evidence · 86

Chapter 11
Organizational Structure of Forensic Science

Category of Forensic Labs · 90
Role of Forensic Science Laboratory · 90
Total Central Labs of Forensic Science in India · 91
Total State Labs of Forensic Science in India · 91
Hierarchy of Lab Administration · 93
Division in Forensic Science Laboratory · 94

Chapter 12
Case Studies

Cases on Importance of Forensic report in Indian court · 102
Cases solved by Forensic Tools · 104

References

@forensicfield

Chapter 1

▶ Introduction

- ▶ What is Forensic Science?
- ▶ Is Criminalistics and Forensic Same?
- ▶ What is Criminology?
- ▶ Main Ingredients of Forensic Science
- ▶ History of Forensic Science
- ▶ Future of Forensic Science
- ▶ Scope of Forensic Science
- ▶ Need of Forensic Science
- ▶ What is use of Forensic Science?
- ▶ How Reliable Is Forensic Science?
- ▶ Reel Vs. Reality

What is Forensic Science?

Forensic Science is a Latin term which is a combination of Forensic and Science, where **Forensis** means a place or meeting where people discuss their ideas.

Forensic science is a cluster of science where scientific methods and processes helps to solve crime cases, civil cases as well as disputed matter also.

Generally it is defined as the application of scientific methods and techniques to matters under investigation by a court of law.

Is Criminalistics and Forensic Same?

Whether both are different titles but work is same. They both investigate crime-scene. Identification, analysis and examination of physical evidences are done by both.

In other words, they are same with different names. They are part of each other. Some time it is known as Criminalistics and some time as forensic science.

What is Criminology?

Criminology is an area of Sociology that mainly focuses on the study of crimes, causes of crime, its effect on society.

Criminology's main focus is to study the behaviour of criminal.

Criminologist takes interest for understanding the base and causes of crime and its effect on society.

Main Ingredients of Forensic Science

✓ **Crime** – A crime is an unlawful act punishable by a state or other authorities.

✓ **Crime-Scene** - A crime scene is physical location, where a Crime occurs.

✓ **Criminal** - Criminal is, relating to, involving, or being a crime. Or who commits crime is Criminal.

✓ **Chain of Custody** - The whole process or movement location of physical evidence from the time it is obtained until the time it is presented in court.

✓ **Evidences** - The available body of facts or information indicating on which to base proof or to establish truth or falsehood.

✓ **Suspect** – Suspect is a person who thought to be guilty of a crime or offence.

✓ **Victim** – Victim is a person who is harmed, injured, or killed as a result of a crime, accident, or other event or action.

✓ **Drugs** - A drug is any substance that causes a change in an organism's physical or mental health when consumed.

✓ **Illegal** - contrary to or forbidden by law, especially criminal law.

✓ **Justice** - Justice, in its broadest context, includes both the attainment of that which is just and the philosophical discussion of that which is just.

✓ **Police** - The police are a constituted body empowered by a state to enforce the law, to protect the citizens, and to prevent crime.

- Fingerprint marks have been used as signature identification for illiterate people since centuries.

- In 1775, A Swedish Chemist **"Carl Wilhelm Scheele"** devised the first successful test for detecting arsenic in corpse and later the work is expanded by German Chemist *"Valentin Rose"*. He discovered method for detection of small amount of arsenic poison in the walls of stomach.

- In 1814, **Mathieu Joseph Bonaventure Orfila** published first scientific treatise on the detection of poison and their effects on animals. He was a Spanish toxicologist and chemist, also known as **Father of Toxicology**. He worked to make chemical analysis a part of forensic medicine.

- In 1835, **Calvin Hooker Goddard** pioneered the use of bullet comparison. He examined the bullet casings in 1929 St. Valentines Day Massacre and showed that the guns used were not police issued weapons, which concluded that the bullet was not official, it was hit by a mob. Calvin Goddard also known as **Father of Forensic Ballistics**.

- **Alphonse Bertillon** was the first to use fingerprints to solve crime. His Anthropometric method identifying criminals represented a first step toward scientific criminology. Alphonse Bertillon was the first to apply the anthropological technique of anthropometry to law enforcement. He devised a system of identification of criminals which also known as **"Bertillon System"** which relies on 11 bodily measurements in 1879. He explained his system in his book **"Photography: With an Appendix on Anthropometrical Classification and Identification"**. He was also a **First Forensic Photographer**.

- Around 1850s and 1860s, at the time of working in India **William J. Herschel** started to use fingerprints and handprints as a signature. In 1916, William James Herschel published his Book named as **"The Origin of Fingerprinting"**. In which he shared all his experiences with fingerprints.

→ In 1880, **Henry faulds** published a paper on how to catch criminals by fingerprints in **"Nature"** magazine. Henry Faulds was the first who suggest fingerprints for forensic use.

→ **Francis Galton** was the first who studied about fingerprints and uses of it on a scientific basis. He published 3 booklets in the row :

▶ **Fingerprints** in 1892

▶ **Blurred Fingerprints** in 1893

▶ **Fingerprints Directories** in 1895

→ *Galton* also published many papers and articles on fingerprints.

→ In 1893, **Juan Vucetich** published his first book on "General Instructions for the Anthropometric System and Fingerprints". Juan Vucetich created an apparatus to take fingerprints which was known as **"Dactiloscopic Table"**.

→ In 1893, **Hans Gross** published his book entitled as **"Manuals for Investigators, Police Officials and gendarmes"**. In 1902, he published his 2nd book named as "**Criminal Psychology**". Hans Gross published a book "**Criminal Investigation (Handbuch fur Untersuchungsrichter als System der Kriminalistik)**" in 1893 to make up for deficiency in criminalistics.

→ **Dr. Edmond Locard** formulated the basic principle of forensic science which is "**Every Contact Leaves a Trace**". This principle also known as Locard's exchange principle. Locard's paper "**Lenquete Criminelle et les Methods Scientifique**" in 1904 published a phrase "Every Contact Leaves a Trace". He also known as the "**Sherlock Holmes of France**".

→ **Albert Sherman Osborn** was the first who introduced questioned document examination and forged document analysis. In 1910, he wrote a book on "**Questioned Documents**". In 1937 he published another book "**Laymen's View of the Law**".

→ **Walter C. McCrone (1916 – 2002)** Developed advances in microscopic techniques to solve crimes and analyze evidence.

→ **In 1916,** Dr. **Leone Lattes** created a procedure to determine the blood group from dried blood. He also introduced forensic paternity and DNA identification through dried blood stain.

→ **Mark Twain** mentioned identification of murder by fingerprint identification.

→ **Luke May** developed tool mark striation analysis and observation and published his work in American Journal of Police Science in 1930.

→ In 1863, A German Scientist named **Christian Schonbein** discovered the **first Preliminary test for blood.**

→ In 1879, A German Scientist **Rudolph Virchow** had **first described the unique characteristics of Hair.**

→ A French Physician "*Francois-Emanuel Fodere*" wrote "**A treatise on Forensic Medicine and public health**" in 1978. It was a First Treatise on Forensic Science for understanding of working of the body.

→ The development of National DNA Index System created by the FBI in 1998.

Indian History of Forensic Science

→ Indian studied various patterns of papillary line thousands year ago. As we have discussed above about use of fingerprint as a signature by **William James Herschel.**

→ Gradually, need of forensics also felt by law enforcement agencies of India. In the way of that following laboratories and branches were developed.

→ The first Chemical examination laboratory was established in Chennai in **1849**.

→ In **1853**, the second chemical examination laboratory established in Kolkata.

→ 3rd chemical examination laboratory is established in Agra in **1864**.

→ 4th chemical examination laboratories established in **1870** in Mumbai.

→ Anthropometry Bureau was first established in Kolkata in **1892**. It was based on Bertillon's system.

→ First explosive examination laboratory was developed in Nagpur in **1898**.

→ The first Government Examiner of Questioned Document is established in Bengal in 1904 and shifted to Shimla in **1906**.

→ After the recommendations of the Royal Police Commission in 1902-03, the first Central Finger Print Bureau (CFPB) in India was established in **1905** at Shimla.

- Establishment of Serology Department by **Dr. Hankin** in Kolkata in **1910**.

- During the year **1915**, a Footprint Section was established under the CID, Government of Bengal.

- In **1917** by government of Bengal, Note Forgery Section had been developed under the CID, Government of Bengal, to undertake the examination of forged currency notes.

- For examination of Narcotic Substance along with liquor analysis and estimation of purity lab of precious metal like Gold, Silver, etc. Government of Bengal started its own laboratory.

- In **1930**, an Arms Expert was appointed and a small ballistic laboratory was set up under the Calcutta Police to deal with the examination of firearms.

- During **1936**, a Scientific Section was set up under the CID in Bengal and facilities were created for examination of bullets, cartridge cases, firearms, etc., used in committing crime.

- The question of introducing criminology and forensic science as the courses of study at the university level in India was taken up with the Vice-Chancellors of various universities during **1950**, but the progress made in this direction was not encouraging.

- The first state forensic science laboratory in India was established in the year **1952** at Calcutta.

- Central detective training school at Calcutta, in India, was established during **1956** and was located (in the same premises) with the CFPB, Calcutta.

- Fingerprint bureau also established in Kolkata in first place in **1957** by Khan Bhadur Aziz ulla haq and Ray

Bahadur Khem Chandra Bose. They both had contributed a lot for this bureau.

→ The first Central Forensic Science Laboratory was established at Calcutta during **1957**.

→ The Union Government, during **1959**, appointed two committees for the purpose of giving a lead to all the States in establishing new forensic science laboratories and improving the existing ones, and for improving the study and application of Forensic Medicine.

→ The Indian Academy of Forensic Sciences (IAFS) was established in the year **1960**.

→ The Institute of Criminology and Forensic Science (ICFS) was established in Delhi during **1971** with the limited objectives of imparting training to the in-service personnel and conducting research in Criminology and Forensic Science.

→ The Central Detective Training School, Hyderabad was established in **1964**, on the pattern of the CDTS, Calcutta, followed by another one at Chandigarh, during **1973**.

→ After rising demands of providing high technology and techniques to the crime investigation process, BPR&D established the first Forensic DNA Typing facility at CFSL, Calcutta, during **1998**.

Future of Forensic Science

There has always been a role for forensic science from years back in criminal investigations. Day by day forensic expert come up with new technologies and techniques to solve crime and catch criminals but criminals are also coming up with their own unique styles to commit crime. And for each and every crime forensic experts need to adapt different manners. As world is being digital access of information is much easier to anyone which is also helping criminals to commit crime more, because of that forensic field also need to expand its criteria, technologies, methods and men power for investigation of crime in future so that criminal stop misusing techno world. So talking about future of forensics is not going to end soon.

➔ "If There Is Human There Is Crime And If There Is Crime There Is Forensics"

➔ "We do not catch criminals, we identify them."

By Archana Singh

Scope of Forensic Science

The Scope of forensic field is vast. Collecting materials from crime scene and analyzing them in lab is a very difficult job. There are lots of opportunities in this field, Such as; forensic expert, forensic scientist, crime scene investigator, lab assistant, etc. besides of these, there are many other options as well, like; teaching, jobs in private firm, Government sector, forensic photographer, working with CBI, crime branch and, many more unlimited options are available in this field. Some listed jobs are following:

- Crime Analyst
- Legal counselors
- Forensic Expert
- Forensic Scientist
- Forensic Odontologist
- Teacher / Professor
- Handwriting Expert
- Crime Scene Investigator
- Forensic Engineer
- Forensic Architects
- Forensic Psychiatrist
- Crime Reporter
- Forensic Toxicologist
- Forensic Serologist

Top Recruiting Areas

- Colleges and Universities,
- Police department,
- Research Laboratories,

- Hospitals,
- Pharmaceutical Companies, etc.

Some places where one can find a job are given below:

- Intelligence Bureau (IB)
- Central Bureau of Investigation (CBI)
- Central Govt. Forensic Sciences Labs
- Law Firms
- Private Detective Agencies
- Hospitals
- Police Department
- Quality Control Bureau
- Universities
- Banks
- Defense/Army

Need of Forensic Science

I. **Changes in Society** – Society is changing very rapidly. Each day is coming up with new challenges and same applies for forensic field. Criminals search new ways to commit crime. Forensic experts also need to come with their new ideas to defeat the criminals.

II. **Technology and Techniques** - Now a days technology are very handy And every day the world is becoming increasingly familiar with new technologies. Criminals are changing their techniques for their wrongdoings. Forensic experts will always have to search for new tools and techniques to solve it.

III. **More Crime More Evidences** – As crime rate is increasing rapidly so new evidences are also being identified and for that forensic expert will also have to discover new methods.

IV. **Growing Crime Rate** – Crime rate is growing with time and population so there is need of forensic science to solve them and catch the criminals in very short time.

V. **Population Growth** – Population is increasing so is crime. So there is a need of forensic as well.

VI. **Others**- The different types of crime causation are as follows;

- Unemployment
- Paternity dispute
- Bribe
- Land Dispute
- Ransom

- Money Dispute
- Illegal Advantages
- Religious Dispute, etc.

For all the above reasons forensic science laboratories need to expand more so that justice will not be delayed and no more pending cases will remain in offices.

Rapid and quick development in forensics will solve crime even faster.

What is Use of Forensic Science?

Most common uses of forensic to investigate criminal cases, Civil Cases or dispute between parties involving a victim and suspect, Such as; document forgery, murder, sexual assault, loot, robbery, abduction, kidnapping, rape, duplicate branding, property dispute, signature forgery, fraud, etc.

Forensic science performs an essential function in the framework of the judicial system by providing data scientifically through the examination of physical evidence. During an examination, evidence is gathered at a crime scene or from an individual, investigated in a forensic science laboratory and after that the outcomes presents in court.

How Reliable Is Forensic Science?

In any case, regularly most criminological proof is helped by fastidious logical examination suggesting that it doesn't generally demonstrate towards the individual who is blameworthy. However there are limitations, a few techniques utilized in the field have numerous restrictions that make us question the practicality of confiding in results. Forensic science is under question for a lack of reliability.

Like the TV shows in where, after committing crime criminal get caught within an hour with clear evidence and their analysis. But real life is very different than reel life. Evidences are not always available. And sometime evidences get contaminated which are not accurate or enough for examination. In real life we do not very much rely on trace evidences without support of other evidences or witnesses. Such as; in reel only a fingerprint is able to catch a criminal while in reality this is circumstantial evidence. That means they are not as reliable as they are shown on TV.

Forensic science laboratories never assured 100% results and therefore labs covered this conclusions with "May be", "Like", "can be", etc.

Forensic Science is growing fast day by day with new techniques and methods. But because of less care of Scene Of Crime, Evidences, lack of man power and right training, it is still less reliable and courts do not rely completely on forensic report for conviction of crime. Forensic evidences only used as a part of argument to prove someone guilty or clean by the advocates but generally, the court doesn't prove guilty or give clean chit to accused only on the basis of forensic evidences.

Reel vs. Reality

While on TV shows, Such as; *CSI*, where Forensic Investigators are seen interviewing witnesses, in "real" life, Forensic Investigators have no contact with witnesses, suspects or others. The role of Forensic Investigators is purely about collection and analysis of evidences and search of the crime scene. It is up to the police to interrogate, and put the pieces of the crime together.

Chapter 2

▶ Law and Forensic Science in India

Law and Forensic Science in India

Indian Evidence Act, 1872

Section 3- Witnesses and Documents are the main sources of evidence in any proceedings. A witness is person gives affidavit or evidence before any Court.

Oral evidence is when evidence given by witnesses.

Documentary evidence is when the evidence produced through the document.

According to Section 3 of the Indian Evidence Act, 1872, documentary evidence means and includes all documents which produced before the Court for its inspection.

Documents are divided into two categories:

Public Documents and *Private Documents.*

Section 3 of **Indian Evidence Act, 1872** defines Document as, "**Document**" means any matter expressed or described on any substance which means letters, figures or marks, or more than one of the means intended to be used, or which may be used, for the purpose of recording that case. "

Section 45- Opinions of experts—

"When the court is required to form an opinion on the point of foreign law or science or art or in the form of identification of handwriting or fingerprints, the opinion of the persons at that point particularly skilled in such foreign law, science or art, Or questions such as handwriting or fingerprint identification are relevant facts, such individuals are called experts."

Illustrations

(a) If the question arises in front of a forensic expert to know his opinion about the death of a person due to poison, the forensic expert will only tell the symptoms of the poison and the type of poison from which that person died.

(b) If a person was unable to know the nature of the work at the time of performing a certain task, due to the unsoundness of mind, or was doing something that was either wrong or contrary to the law. Experts opinion on the question of whether symptoms generally show unsoundness to the mind, and whether such indifference to the mind usually makes individuals unable to understand the nature of the acts that they perform, or knowing that What they do is either wrong or, contrary to the law, relevant.

(c) The question is whether a certain document was written by a person. Another document is produced, which is proved or believed to be written by the same person. The opinion of experts on this question whether the two documents were written by the same person or different persons is relevant.

Section 46- Facts bearing upon opinions of experts —

"Facts that are not otherwise relevant are relevant if they support the opinions of experts or are inconsistent when such opinions are relevant."

Illustrations

(a) The question is whether the person was poisoned by a certain poison. The fact that the other person, who was poisoned by that person, exhibited some symptoms, which experts confirm or deny being symptoms of that poison, is relevant.

COMMENTS- Admissibility, the science of identifying footprints, is not a fully developed science and therefore if in a given case, the evidence related to the same is found to be satisfactory, it can only be used to reinforce the conclusion as the culprit. Identification is already in progress based on other evidence.

Section 65B - Admissibility of electronic records

It deals with the admissibility of electronic records as evidence in court of law.

Notwithstanding anything contained in this Act, any information contained in an electronic record that is stored, recorded or copied on paper in a computer-produced optical or magnetic media (hereinafter referred to as computer output) will also be considered. A document, if the conditions mentioned in this section are satisfied with respect to information and computer and as proof of any material of origin or any fact, shall be admissible in any proceeding without further proof or production of the original. Out of which direct evidence will be acceptable.

Section 73- According to this section, the Indian Evidence Act empowers the court to direct any person, including an accused, to be allowed to take his fingerprints.

"Comparison of signature, writing or seal accepted or certified with others. -

To determine whether the signature, writing or seal belongs to the person by whom it is written or created, any signature, writing, or seal has been accepted or written or proven to the satisfaction of the court. The person may be compared to the person who is to be proved, although that signature, writing, or seal is not produced or proven for any other purpose. The court may direct any person present in the court to write any word or figure for the purpose of enabling the court to compare any words or figures.

This section also applies to fingerprints, with any necessary modifications.

Section 74- According to **Section 74** of Indian Evidence Act, 1872 the Following Documents are Public Documents:

(1) Documents forming the acts, or records of the acts—

(i) Of the sovereign authority,

(ii) Of official bodies and tribunals, and

(iii) Of public officers, legislative, judicial and executive, of any part of India or of the Commonwealth, or of a foreign country;

(2) Public records kept in any State of private documents.

As per Section 75, "all other documents other than those, listed in Section 74 of Indian Evidence Act are Private Documents."

Prevention of Terrorism Act, 2002

Section 27 - Power to direct for samples, etc.

(1) When a police officer investigating a case requests the Court of a Chief Judicial Magistrate or the Court of a Chief Metropolitan Magistrate in writing for obtaining samples of hand writing, finger-prints, foot-prints, photographs, blood, saliva, semen, hair, voice of any accused person, reasonably suspected to be involved in the commission of an offence under this Act, it shall be lawful for the Court of a Chief Judicial Magistrate or the Court of a Chief Metropolitan Magistrate to direct that such samples be given by the accused person to the police officer either through a medical practitioner or otherwise, as the case may be.

Information Technology (Amendment) Act, 2008

Section 79A- Central Government to notify Examiner of Electronic Evidence.

The Central Government may, for the purposes of providing expert opinion on electronic form evidence before any court or other authority specify, by notification in the Official Gazette, any Department, body or agency of the Central Government or a State Government as an Examiner of Electronic Evidence.

Explanation - For the purposes of this section, "electronic form evidence" means information of any possible value that is either stored or transmitted in electronic form and includes computer evidence, digital audio, digital video, cell phones, digital fax machines are included.

Narcotic Drugs and Psychotropic Substances Act, 1985

Section 2- Definition of Chemical Examiner

- ☞ [(c) "Chemical Examiner means the Chemical Examiner or Deputy Chief Chemist or Shift Chemist or Assistant Chemical Examiner. Government Opium and Alkaloid Works, Neemuch or, as the case may be, Ghazipur]

- ☞ Chemical analysis is necessary in case of identification of opium in a mixture.

Chapter 3

- **Eligibility**

- **What Skills Are Involved In Forensic Science?**
- **Eligibility For Forensic Science Courses**

What Skills Are Involved In Forensic Science?

Forensic science uses a lot of different skills. These include:

O Observational skills –

- To be able to find and compare evidence.

- To be able to discover things the untrained eye may miss.

O Evidence collection and analysis –

- This is vital role of a forensic scientist.

- Evidence that is collected needs to be well documented and it is crucial that contamination of evidence does not occur.

- To collect evidence a forensic scientist needs to be methodical and accurate.

O Scepticism –

- Healthy scepticism is an important part of investigating crimes. Everyone is a suspect until something solid proves otherwise.

- It is also important to understand that witness accounts aren't always very accurate.

- It has been found that when referring to memories (Such as; during a witness account) most people have trouble getting all details correct and most people's perceptions are based on their personal lives and values.

Eligibility for Forensic Science Courses

Bachelor of Sciences (B.Sc.)

B.Sc. in forensic science is a 3-year graduate course which involves the application of scientific knowledge to the investigation of crimes.

Eligibility Criteria

To meet the basic criteria of eligibility for admission to the course is a Higher Secondary (10 + 2) or equivalent qualification from a recognized academic board with Physics, Chemistry and Biology or Mathematics as the core subjects and a minimum aggregate score of 55%. For other countries Grade 12 or equivalent with science subjects is need to be qualified.

Admission Process

Admission to the course is based on the candidate's percentage at the 10+2 level (percentage varies with universities). Institutes offering the course accept students on the basis that they achieve the minimum, set cut-off scores at the 10+2 level. Some institutes conduct entrance test for admission at their own level.

M.Sc. in Forensic Science

M.Sc. in Forensic Science is a 2-year full-time post-graduate course which is divided into 4 semesters.

M.Sc. in Forensic Science is designed for both graduate students and forensic practitioners.

Eligibility Criteria

- Minimum eligibility criteria for M.Sc. in Forensic Science course may vary across universities and institutes.

- Primarily, the criteria include:
- Bachelor's degree in science/engineering/ pharmacy/ medicine, obtained from a recognized university.
- A minimum aggregate score of 50-60% at the level of graduation (vary across institutes).

Ph.D. in Forensic Science

Ph.D. in Forensic Science is a Research level program in forensic field. The duration of which ranges from 2 years to 5 years.

Eligibility Criteria

Students seeking admission to Ph.D. in Forensic Science course must hold a Master's degree in relevant discipline or equivalent from a recognized university. Candidates have to clear the cut off marks set by the respective College/ University to get admission to this course.

Chapter 4

Forensic Scientist

- Work of Forensic Scientist
- What Forensic Scientist Don't Do?
- Responsibilities
- What to expect?

Work of Forensic Scientist

- The role of forensic scientists is vital to the criminal justice process.

- Forensic scientists write reports, preserve evidence, testify in court, and discuss evidence collection with attorneys and law enforcement personnel.

- They record findings and collect trace evidence from scene of crime or accidents.

- Forensic scientists analyse, process & examine evidence received or collected from crime scenes and present their findings based on the results of their analyses.

- Forensic scientists also review and supervise the work of assistants.

- They also have to work with law agencies and coordinate with police team.

- They may also be asked to justify their findings or others findings in court.

- The job and duties of a forensic scientist may vary according to the field of interest or specialty.

- Forensic scientists always need to research and develop new forensic techniques and methods.

What Forensic Scientist Don't Do:

Like the TV shows where after committing crime criminal get caught within an hour with clear evidence and their analysis and all done by forensic experts while in the real life forensic experts don't do all those work which are shown in TV shows. Such as;

- Breaking the Doors;
- Solving case alone;
- Catching suspect/criminals;
- Interrogating suspects;
- Psychic Intuition;
- Chasing suspects;
- Checking Alibis;
- They don't go first on the crime scene, etc.

Responsibilities

- Forensic scientist record findings and collect trace evidence from scene of crime.

- Forensic scientist need to analyze samples, such as; hair, body fluids, glass, paint and drugs.

- In the laboratory, they need to apply techniques, Such as; Gas and High-Performance Liquid Chromatography, Scanning Electron Microscopy, Mass Spectrometry, Infrared Spectroscopy and Genetic Fingerprinting.

- They Examine Crime Scene and coordinate with outside agencies, Such as; the police.

- They supervise the work of assistants present at the crime scene.

- They keep their results of work in written form for future use of legal proceedings.

- They also give oral evidence in court after demand of judicial Authority.

- They justify findings under cross-examination in courts of law, research and develop new forensic techniques.

What to Expect?

✓ Normally most of the work is laboratory-based. They need to know about tools and techniques according to their expertise so that they can perform their Job outstandingly.

✓ Experienced forensic scientists may have to attend crime scenes.

✓ Forensic scientist should be prepared for presenting and defending the evidence in court under cross-examination.

✓ They should be innovative and always try to discover new methods and techniques for analysis of evidences.

Chapter 5

▶ Tools & Techniques of Forensic Science

Tools & Techniques of Forensic Science

The instruments and techniques which are utilized for assessment of physical evidences should be characterized into meet the following demands:

- **Sensitivity** – Tools and apparatus should be very sensitive so that they can analyze and examine even small quantity samples or evidences.

  At the time of crime scene investigation evidences can be found anywhere in any quantity. May be it is only a strand of a hair or a drop of blood. Because of the small quantity of evidence it is very necessary to get the result at once.

- **Specificity** – Results given by tools and Instruments should be very specific for their evidentiary value. Because evidences meant to present in court and the process often depends on these result. So result should be very specific.

- **Rapidity** – Instruments, tools or Apparatus should always be ready for another analysis. Because of the increasing crime rate and demand of forensic reports forensic experts need to use tools again and again so their rate of uses should be higher. A result should take as little time as possible.

- **Accuracy** – The result given by the instrument or tool should be accurate for investigation.

  Errors in result may lead to injustice for someone or investigation can be interrupt because of less accurate result.

The Most Common Used Techniques Are Following:

There are lots of techniques and methods used by the forensic scientist and experts. However, there are some most frequently used and common techniques mentioned below:

1. Phenom SEM

The Phenom SEM for Gun Shot Residue allows crime labs to analyze for gunshot residue particles. With the Phenom SEM, sample structures can be physically examined and their elemental composition determined.

2. Alternative Light Photography

This is used to detect whether damage has been done to a body. The camera used blue light and orange filters to see whether bruising has occurred below the skin's surface.

3. Facial Reconstruction

This equipment is used by many forensic labs to determine the appearance of victims who are too decomposed or damaged to make a visual identification. The user inputs data into the software, including information regarding human remains, and a possible physical appearance is deduced.

4. DNA Sequencing

DNA is used to identify both criminals and victims by using trace evidence, Such as; hair or skin.

5. Automated Fingerprint Identification

There are many techniques used to identify fingerprints. Some of new technologies, Such as; magnetic fingerprinting dust are able to get a perfect impression of fingerprint without messing the prints.

6. Link Analysis Software

Link Analysis Software is used to highlights any strange financial activity found within the paper trail.

7. Drug Testing

Forensic teams are often requested to identify unknown substances for their standards or for identification. Labs use Color Testing, Ultraviolet Spectrophotometry, Gas Chromatography, Microcrystalline Testing, etc. to confirm type of drugs, its composition, etc.

8. Laser Ablation Inductively Coupled Plasma Mass Spectrometry (LA-ICP-MS)

The Laser Ablation Inductively Coupled Plasma Mass Spectrometry (LA-ICP-MS) helps put minutest pieces of glass back together. This also helps in determine the direction of bullets, force of impact or even the type of weapon used in a crime.

9. Mass Spectrometers

Mass spectrometers are used to analyze trace evidence by determining the composition of substances and elements.

10. High-Powered Microscopes

Microscope is a very important and most necessary part of forensic laboratory. With the help of high-powered microscopes, these tiny pieces of evidence can be viewed more clearly and can thus be more easily identified.

11. Chromatography

Chromatography is used to separate mixtures of their individual components to identify them correctly.

12. Various Cameras and Photography Techniques

Photography, or "writing or drawing with light", is defined as the processor art of producing images of objects on sensitized surfaces by the chemical action of light or of other forms of radiant energy, Such as; X-rays, Gamma rays or cosmic rays.

Fixing an image permanently has been possible since the 1820s in different ways, such as; from the daguerreotype, to silver plates, to film and now digitally.

Alternative light, UV photography, high-speed ballistics photography, etc. helps to reconstruct crime scene through the images.

For the convenience of forensic scientist, many more techniques are being introduced day by day by experts so that they can identify, analyze and examine evidence, samples etc. in a short time.

Chapter 6

▶ Branches of Forensic Science

Branches of Forensic Science

Forensic Science is an applied science. It is the study of scientific principles used to solve crimes and help judiciary systems. It derives its principles and techniques from basic sciences that's why it has various number of branches.

Forensic science can be further classified into a number of branches:

▪ Criminalistics

Criminalistics is the application of science which uses to collect, examine, identify and compare evidences, such as; biological, trace, ballistics, impression evidence and other related to investigation.

▪ Forensic Biology

Forensic biology section examines evidence for the presence of body fluids, such as; blood, semen, saliva, DNA analysis, etc.

▪ Forensic Chemistry

Under forensic chemistry detection, recognition and examination of illicit drugs, explosives and gunshot residue are identified and analyzed. Basically this branch deals with all the tests to detect the presence of various chemicals.

▪ Forensic Physics

In this branch of forensic science we study buildings, ballistics, bombs, blood spatters, soil, glass, fiber, etc.

▪ Forensic Document Examination

Questioned document examination is set of standard procedure for comparison and identification of original and forge document, signature, disputed wills and official papers.

▪ Forensic Pathology

In the branch of pathology a corpse test is performed to determine the cause of death.

▪ Forensic Psychology

Forensic psychology is the application of psychology to legal and criminal matters.

Forensic psychologists study criminals and their crimes that draw conclusions about the personality traits of the perpetrators and thus assist in criminal profiling.

▪ Forensic Toxicology

Forensic toxicology is the study of poisons and drugs. In toxicology, the presence of toxic substance inside a body and their effects on a person is analyzed and investigated.

▪ Forensic Botany

Forensic botany is the study and examination of plant-based evidence. Such as; leaves, flowers, wood, fruits, seeds, pollen.

▪ Forensic Serology

The study of viscera and various body fluids, such as; blood, semen, vaginal secretion, vomit, sweat, urine, etc.

- **Forensic Ballistics**

Forensic ballistics involves the analysis of any evidence related to firearms (bullets, bullet marks, shell casings, gunpowder residue etc.).

- **Trace Evidence Analysis**

Going by locard's principle that "every contact leaves traces", trace evidence analysis provides crucial links to the perpetrator. Trace evidence is anything that is transferred during the commission of a crime, such as; human/animal hair, rope, soil, fabric fibers, feathers, building materials etc.

- **Forensic Podiatry**

Forensic podiatry deals with the application of specific podiatric knowledge, i.e., an understanding of the abnormalities and diseases of the ankle, foot, and lower body, and lower limb anatomy, and musculoskeletal function. This is particularly helpful in the investigation of foot-based evidence with respect to a criminal incident.

- **Forensic Odontology**

Forensic odontology is also known as study of teeth involves the proper handling, analysis, and evaluation of any form of dental evidence that would be later used as legal evidence in the court of law. Criminal investigations comprising bite marks largely involve the discipline of forensic odontology.

- **Forensic Medicine**

Forensic medicine science is related to autopsy, post-mortem, ante-mortem, peri-mortem examination.

▪ Forensic Entomology

Forensic entomology involves the application and study of insects and other arthropods to solve criminal cases. It uses insects within and surrounding human remains to determine the time or place of death by examination.

▪ Forensic Linguistics

Forensic linguistics includes linguistic knowledge and methods of criminal investigations and judicial proceedings. It's involved in the examination of forensic texts, such as; emergency calls, demands of ransom, suicide notes, social media and death row statements.

▪ Forensic Geology / Geoforensics

Forensic geology or geoforensics deals with the examination of evidence related to materials found in the earth, such as; oil, petroleum, minerals, soil, rocks and the lake.

▪ Forensic Engineering

It involves the application of engineering principles to the investigation and analysis of such mechanical and structural failures. Such as; building and bridges collapse and similar things.

▪ Forensic DNA Analysis

It is used in criminal investigations, comparing the criminal, suspect's profile to DNA evidence to establish their involvement in the crime. It also used to determine family relationship and identify disasters victims. The biological evidence used for DNA profiling include hair, skin, semen, urine, blood, saliva and even body remains in burn cases.

▪ Forensic Archeology

Such techniques along with the use of photography and imaging enable forensic archeologists to assist the police and investigating officers to identify the site where the victim's body and personal items, or robbed goods are buried.

▪ Forensic Anthropology

Under this branch, bones, skeletons of humans or animals are analyzed through recovery and examination. Forensic anthropologists examine human bodies/skeletons to help identify the individuals and reach the cause of death.

▪ Digital Forensics

It is mostly used in the investigation of cybercrimes. This branch mainly deals with the cyber-crimes and online frauds etc.

▪ Forensic Dactyloscopy

Forensic fingerprint is the study of fingerprints.

▪ Forensic Accounting

Forensic accounting is the study and analysis of accounting evidence.

Chapter 7

▶ Laws and Principles of Forensic Science

Laws and Principles of Forensic Science

Forensic Science is the science that has developed its own Laws and Principles. The Laws and Principles of all the basic sciences are the base of Forensic Science. Every object, natural or man-made, has an individuality which is not duplicated in any other objects.

Laws and Principles of forensic science have been given below:

1. Law of Individuality

Everything involved in a crime, has individuality. If the same is established, it connects the crime and also the criminal.

This principle initially seems to be contrary to common beliefs and observations. The grains of sand or common salt, seeds of plants or twins look alike.

2. Principle Of Exchange

"**Contact exchange traces**" is principle of exchange. It had been first presented by the French scientist, Edmond Locard usually called as Edmond Locard's maxim on Interchange.

According to the principle, once a criminal or his instruments of crime has been in contact with the victim or the nearby objects, they leave traces. Likewise, the criminal or his instruments obtain traces from the same contact.

3. Law Of Progressive Change

"Change is inexorable", this line also applies to criminal, Things or Objects. Different types of objects may take different time spans. The criminal undergoes progressive changes. If he is not getting in time, he becomes unrecognizable. The crime scene undergoes rapid changes.

Changing of weather, various vegetable growth, and the living organism make extensive changes in very short periods.

Samples also degrade with time, Bodies decompose, tire tracks & bite marks fade, the firearm barrel loosen, metal objects rust, etc.

4. Principle of Comparison

Principle of comparison is:

"Only the likes can be compared"

It also emphasized the need to provide samples and specimens for comparisons with the questioned items. A questioned hair can only be compared to known hair sample, same with other marks, such as; tool marks, bite marks, tire marks, etc.

For example –

- ✓ A specimen obtained by writing on the same wall, at the same height and with the same instrument and then photographed. It can be matched.

- ✓ Once handwriting available on a photograph allegedly written on a wall was compared with the specimen written on paper. It did not give worthwhile results.

5. Principle Of Analysis

Principle of Analysis works best for the sample analyzing. Analysis cannot be done if sampling of evidences or specimens is not handled properly or contaminated. This Principle is effective when sample of evidences and others objects or things which need to be analyzed are in the proper and correct packaging. For best analysis of the samples, the samples should be kept in good place and separated from each other.

6. Law Of Probability

All recognizable proof, definite or uncertain, is made, consciously or unconsciously, on the basis of probability. Probability is mostly misunderstood. If we say that according to probability a particular fingerprint has come from the given source, but it is not a definite opinion.

Probability is a scientific idea. It determines the chances of occurrence of a particular event in a particular way.

If "P" = probability, "Ns" = the number of ways in which the event can successfully occur and "Nf" = the number of ways in which it can fail, the probability of success is given by the formula:

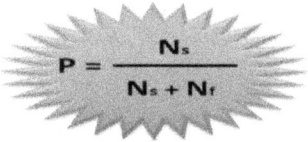

$$P = \frac{N_s}{N_s + N_f}$$

7. Law Of Circumstantial Facts

"Facts Do Not Lie, Men Can And Do"

Evidences given by an eye witnesses or victims may not always be precise. Sometimes victims may purposefully lie or sometimes because of poor senses (Such as; low sight, unclear hearing), misrepresentation & suspicions.

As per Karl Marx "True belief only becomes knowledge when backed by some sort of investigation and evidence".

Chapter 8

▶ Investigation of the Crime Scene

- What is crime scene?
- Investigation team of crime - scene
- How is it possible to identify the person who committed a crime?
- Who is a crime scene investigator?
- Purpose of investigation
- Types of crime scene
- Identifying, establishing, protecting, and securing the boundaries
- Documenting the scene and evidence
- responsibilities of lead investigator
- Systematically search for evidence

Investigation of the Crime Scene

What Is Crime Scene?

A crime scene is a location where crime has been committed.

Crime Scene Investigation

Investigation of the place of the crime is called investigation of the crime scene or crime scene investigation. Crime scene investigation is multidisciplinary and multitasking which involves a systematic and planned search of the crime scene.

Investigation Team of Crime - Scene

The crime scene investigation team consists a group of professional investigators trained in variety of special subjects.

Team Members

- First Police Officer on the scene

- Medics (if necessary)

- Investigators

- Medical Examiner (if necessary)

- Photographer and/or Field Evidence Technician

- Lab Experts. Such as; Pathologist, Document And Handwriting Experts, Fingerprint Expert, Serologist, Firearm Examiner, DNA Expert, Toxicologist.

How is it possible to identify the person who committed a crime?

☞ A little amount of blood or a hair or a fiber or a part of skin or any number of different types of materials can help a crime to be reconstructed and lead investigators to the accused.

☞ The goal of a crime-scene investigation is to recognize, document and collect evidence at the scene of a crime.

☞ Solving the crime depends on putting together the evidence to form a picture of what happened at the location of crime.

Investigative Process is to:

☞ Establish that a crime was actually committed,

☞ Identify and apprehend the suspect,

☞ Identification and analysis of the evidences.

☞ Recover stolen property,

☞ Assistance in the prosecution of the person and in proving the charge of crime.

Who is a Crime Scene Investigator?

A crime scene investigator is generally a member of law enforcement agency, which is responsible to maintain law and order and to catch criminals. They investigate crime scene by identifying, collecting, preserving, and packaging evidences.

Purpose of Investigation:

The purpose of criminal investigation and forensic science is to discover the truth behind the scene.

The purpose of crime scene investigation is to investigate and establish that:

- What happened?
- What was the reason?
- Who did it?
- How it happened?
- Who is affected?
- Where is the base of crime? etc.

These some above questions are the examples of purpose of crime scene investigation.

Types of Crime Scene

❖ Outdoor Crime Scene

❖ Indoor Crime Scene

❖ Outdoor - Indoor Crime Scene

❖ Conveyances

❖ **Outdoor Crime Scene-**

When crime occurred at open place then that place is known as Outdoor Crime Scene. It is very difficult to find evidences at an outdoor crime scene because these are very easily destroyed due to external interference, so these need immediate attention and processing to secure the place.

For Ex- Riot between communities, murder at open space, Hit & Run, explosion etc.

❖ **Indoor Crime Scene–**

When crime occurred at closed space then that place is called as Indoor Crime Scene. Evidences may be more available at an Indoor Crime Scene than at an outdoor crime scene.

For Ex- Dowry death, Theft, Burglary, Homicide.

❖ **Outdoor-Indoor Crime Scene-**

When Crime took place partially in closed space and partially at the open place then it's called Outdoor Indoor

Crime Scene. This type of crime scene also needs to be protected immediately due to the probability of evidence being destroyed.

For Ex- Murder in house and disposed of body in river, etc.

- ❖ **Conveyance**-

Conveyance is a means of transportation.

Any crime committed in transport falls in this category. Such as;

- Vehicle burglary.
- Used vehicle in Grand theft.
- Car theft.

The Probability of finding evidence at this type of crime scene is highly positive because suspect may leave evidences in hurry. A conveyance, Such as; a car, may be transported to the laboratory after completion of proper documentation.

Identifying, Establishing, Protecting, and Securing the Boundaries:

→ The initial Boundary established around the crime scene should be larger than the scene.

→ This boundary can easily be shifted inward later but not easily extended outward because the surroundings areas may have been contaminated during ensuring gaps.

→ The responding officer's must document all actions and observations at the scene as soon as possible.

How to Secure Crime Scene?

- Naturally, a general rule of protecting the crime scene cannot be applied in every case.

- Who arrive first at crime scene referred as first officer or first responder. The first officer's top priority to offer assistance for any injured person.

- To safeguards evidence and minimize contamination, access to scene must be limited and any persons found at the scene must be identified, documented and then removed from the scene.

- As additional officers arrive, they will begin procedures to isolate the area, using barricades and police tape to keep away unauthorized persons from the scene.

The first officer should note the following Points:

1. The overall state and condition of the scene upon arrival:

- Doors — open, closed or locked? On which side was the key?

- Windows — open or closed? Were they locked?

- Lights — on or off? Which lights were on?

- Shades, shutters or blinds — open or closed?

- Odors — cigarette, smoke, gas, gun powder, perfume, etc.?

- Signs of activity — meal preparation, dishes in the sink, house clean or dirty, etc.?

- Date and time indicators — mail, newspapers, dates on milk cartons, stopped Clocks, spoiled foods, items that should have been hot or cold but were at room temperature.

2. All personal information concerning witnesses, victims, and suspects.

3. Actions and statements of witnesses, victims and suspects.

4. Moved items condition and their original position (moved item should not be replaced on their original position).

5. All physical evidence should be preserved for identification, collection and submission later.

6. The investigator will establish and safeguards the chain of custody after identifying all persons who entered or exited the scene and documenting all the condition.

7. **Chain of custody** is the sequential documentation or series of a paper that records everything related to the case and maintain for judicial proceedings. It contains sequence of **custody**, control, transfer, analysis, and disposition of physical or electronic evidence.

Evidence Inventory Label

Case # _____   Inventory # _____
Item #   Item description
_____   _____
_____   _____
_____   _____

Date of recovery _____   Time of recovery _____
Location of recovery _____
Recovered by _____
Suspect _____
Victim _____
Type of offense _____

        Chain of custody

Received from _____   By _____
Date _____   Time _____ AM or PM
Received from _____   By _____
Date _____   Time _____ AM or PM
Received from _____   By _____
Date _____   Time _____ AM or PM
Received from _____   By _____
Date _____   Time _____ AM or PM

Documenting the Scene and Evidence:

Documenting of the crime scene and the evidence involve five major tasks:

1. Note-taking
2. Mapping
3. Photography
4. Sketching
5. Videography

1. Note-Taking – The notebook is the investigator's personal reference to record investigations.

The accepted parameters of a police notes and notebooks are:

- A book with a cover page that shows investigators name, date on which notebook was started, and the date notebook was concluded.

- Sequential page numbers.

- A bound booklet from which pages cannot be torn without detection.

- Lined pages that allow for neat scripting of notes.

- Time, date, and case reference should mention in starting of each entry of notebook.

- Blank spaces on pages should not be left between entries and, if a blank space is left, it should be filled or cut with a single line drawn through the space or a diagonal line drawn across a page or partial page space.

- Any errors made in notebook should only be crossed out with a single line drawn through error, and this should not be done in a manner that makes error illegible.

2. Crime Scene Mapping — Mapping is the term used for crime scene measurements. This step is also known as measuring. There are different types used for mapping a crime scene,

There are some basic types of mapping methods use for crime scene sketching and mapping which are:

(A) Baseline,

(B) Rectangular Coordinates,

(C) Triangulation, And

(D) Polar/Grid Coordinates.

(A) **Baseline Mapping** — This is the most accurate and basic method. In this method, a baseline is developed or identified to conduct measurements. Crime scene can be an existing area, Such as; the edge of a roadway, a wall, fence, etc., or it can be developed by Investigators, Such as; by placing a string or tape.

(B) **Rectangular Coordinate Mapping** — This method is more accurate method than baseline method because it utilizes two such baselines instead of one. This method is more accurate than single line baseline method due to two measurements technique. This method is especially useful in confined spaces and smaller interior scenes. Such as; a room, cabin, etc.

(C) **Triangulation Mapping** — This is the most accurate method that does not use advanced technology. While it is quite a bit more laborious and time-consuming, it is sufficiently more accurate than the aforementioned methods of mapping.

(D) **Polar/Grid Coordinate Mapping**— In order to conduct measurements by this method a transit or compass is necessary to measure the angles and polar directions. This method is best used in large outdoor scenes with very few landmarks (e.g., a plane crash in forest or large field).

- **Advanced Mapping Techniques**—Some departments may have the ability to make better utilization of modern technology, Such as; global positioning systems (GPS) and Total Stations, which are mapping systems that can take measurements in polar coordinates and then convert the measurements into grid coordinates.

3. Sketching - there are two types of sketches are produced for documentation of crime scene:-

- *Rough Sketches*

- *Final Sketches*

Sketching is important to crime scene documentation because:

- It accurately portrays the physical facts.

- Sketches of crime scene relates to the sequence of events at the scene.

- It establishes the precise location and relation of objects with crime scene and evidence at the scene.

- It helps to create a mental picture of the scene for those who are not there.

- Crime scene sketch is a permanent record of the scene for further proceedings.

- It usually is admissible in court.

- It assists in interviewing and interrogating.

- It helps investigators for preparing the written investigative report.

- It assists in presenting the case in court. Well-prepared sketches and drawings help judiciary, juries, witnesses, and others to visualize the crime scene.

Investigators can easily recall a crime scene with the help of sketches, and reconstruct entire crime scene into perspective, and with photographs it can provide a much clearer idea of the overall investigation, as well as to point out individual pieces of evidence of crime scene, for example- A bird's eye view sketch of a crime scene enables the investigator to take in the entire scene in one time.

4. Photography - Before anything is touched at crime scene it must be photographed. That will go for the victim and everything found at the crime scene. From minute evidences to the larger one everything should capture. That means something as small as a hair or as large as a sofa.

To effectively review a crime scene, and to view the entire crime scene and accompanying photographs, the representative may give a more clear idea of the general examination, such as evidence at crime scene to indicate individual bits..

Different Type of Photographic Techniques

- Ultra Violet Photography

- Fluorescence Photography

- Infrared Photography

- Macro photography
- Digital Photography
- Panoramic photography
- Multiple Exposure

❖ Ultraviolet Photography

There are two different techniques of ultraviolet photography:

1. Reflected or direct method
2. Ultraviolet fluorescence method

❖ Reflected or direct method

- The reflected ultraviolet photographic technique records solely ultraviolet radiation, within the region 320nm to 390nm, reflected from the subject.
- All different radiation is prevented from reaching the film.
- A source of ultraviolet is directed at the subject which is able to reflect this radiation back to the camera.
- Some materials which are black in visible light reflect ultraviolet thus effectively that they record as white using the reflected ultraviolet Technique.
- Many subjects have a totally different look once viewed via reflected ultraviolet photography.

❖ Fluorescent Photography

- Requires, usually, tripod, remote shutter release, and barrier filter with standard 35mm camera.

- Usually requires about 15-30 seconds time exposure with 35mm.

- Orange 18 is good all-around filter.

- For this type of photography photographer should consider digital camera with barrier filter for real time photos.

❖ **Infrared Photography**

- Infrared techniques are applied within the field or in laboratory surroundings.

- In some instances the only opportunity to document the evidence is in the field at the crime scene.

❖ **Macro Photography**

- Macro photography is extreme close-up photography. It is used to take pictures of very small subjects. This type of photography captures the small subjects into a larger image.

- However in different uses it refers to a finished photograph of a subject at larger than life size.

- A "true" macro photograph is a lot of much outlined as a photograph with a vertical subject height of 24 mm or less.

❖ **Digital Photography**

- Digital photography uses cameras containing arrays of electronic photo detectors to capture pictures centered by a lens, as opposed to an exposure on photographic film.

- Digital cameras within the range of eight to fourteen megapixels can record an equivalent level of fine details in a footwear impression as recorded on a 35mm negative.

❖ Panoramic Photography

- Panoramic photography captures pictures with wide areas with the help of special tools or software.

- It is also known as wide format photography because of its specification.

❖ Multiple Exposure

- In photography and motion-picture photography, a multiple exposure is the superimposition of two or more exposures to create a single image.

- Double exposure contains a corresponding which means in respect of 2 images.

- The exposure values might or might not be the image of one another.

5. **Videography** – Overall videography of crime scene is also important, so that if anything or place have left during sketching or photography then it can be seen in whole crime scene videography.

When a videographer arrives at the scene, an overall view of the area should be recorded, both close up and using a wide angle, with a representative from law enforcement team providing information about date, time, location, case number and other pertinent facts about the case.

Close-up video can be taken to capture the smaller pieces of evidence, with scale or standard-sized items placed nearby to provide scale.

Responsibilities of Lead Investigator:

- The first task of the lead investigator's is that the scene should be processed for physical evidence.

- The collection and analysis should be processed for physical evidence.

- The lead investigator will start with the recognition of physical evidences then supervise and control the processing of crime scene.

- The investigator who protects and searches a crime scene plays a significant role in determining of what will help to solve a crime and which physical evidences will be used to solve the crime and catch the culprit.

Systematically Search For Evidence:

There are several methods used by law enforcement agencies throughout the world. Generally following six basic crime scene search patterns are used:

1. Strip method

2. Wheel method

3. Spiral method

4. Zone method

5. Grid method

6. Line method

The use of any or a number of these search methods will be determined by the location and size of the particular crime scene; the one that is chosen is less important than the fact that the search is carried out with due diligence and attention to detail.

1. **Strip Method** - Strip method requires that crime scene investigator walk a path from one end of the crime scene to the other side of the room or area, and then return in the direction from which he or she first started. Every lap brings the investigator closer to the center of the room or space being searched.

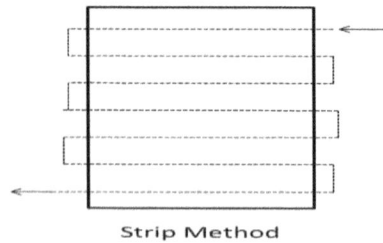

Strip Method

2. **Wheel Method** - The wheel method needs number of crime scene searchers or investigator. It Starting from the middle of an imaginary circle made by investigating officers, each investigator moves in a direction straight out from the center, however, in this method chances of destroying evidences are very much because of the involvement of lots of persons/investigators and lots of paths.

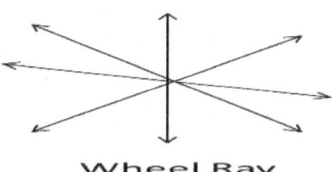

Wheel Ray

3. **Spiral Method-** In this method investigator examining the area for evidence in a more widening circle, search begins at the position of the focal point of the crime scene and then moves in an outward direction. This type of methods takes time.

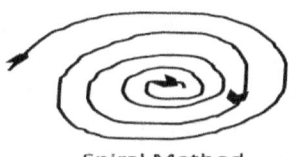

Spiral Method

4. **Zone Method** – In **zone method** investigating officer divides crime scene area into squares. For example, a living room can be divided into four equal sections and examined by an individual investigator. In many cases, those squares are further divided into additional, smaller squares to facilitate evidence location which makes work easier and more searchable.

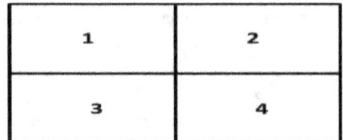

Zone Method

5. Grid Method - The **grid method** is best used in large crime scenes, Such as; fields or woods. Several investigators, or a number of them, move alongside each other from one end of the area to another part of the area.

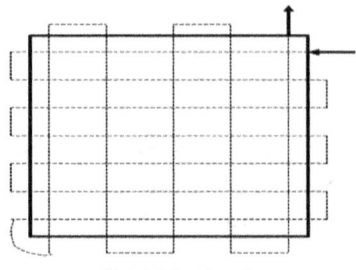

Grid Method

6. Line Method - The **line method** is best used outdoors as well, and is similar to the grid search with the exception that searchers generally only move in one direction, from one side of the search area to the other.

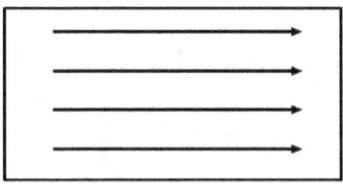

Line Method

As always, remember that the search for any type of evidence starts and ends with the protection and preservation of the crime scene.

Chapter 9

▶ MODUS OPERANDI

- ▶ What is Modus Operandi?
- ▶ Why Modus Operandi Is Used?
- ▶ What Is Modus Operandi Bureau?
- ▶ Types Of Modus Operandi
- ▶ History Of Modus Operandi
- ▶ How Modus Operandi Bureau Solves Crime?
- ▶ Functions Of Modus Operandi Bureau

What is Modus Operandi?

Modus operandi in brief 'MO' is a Latin Term meaning "***A methodology Of Operating***".

Why Modus Operandi Is Used?

It is used by law enforcement Agencies to refer to a criminal pattern of behavior or his/ her manner of committing crime.

What Is Modus Operandi Bureau (MOB)?

This branch collects data of modus operandi of Crime and maintains the records like well-known Criminal Register, History Sheet Register, Guilty Persons Registered and MCR. With this data it helps the investigation officers by giving suggestion with relevancy of the offenders probably to be involved in offences.

Types of Modus Operandi (MO)

- ✓ Selection of the place of Offence.
- ✓ Selection of weapon to commit an offence.
- ✓ Precautions taken by offender.
- ✓ Offender transportation for Crime scene and from Crime scene.

History of Modus Operandi (MO)

→ In 1829 Sir Robert Peel set the foundations of modern police organizations, in which separate task performed by a different group of men specially trained in their work.

- It wasn't till the latter part of the nineteenth century that detective bureau was organized in Europe and America.

- In the last of 1800s century modus operandi Bureau started to include photography into the Criminal Investigation method.

- By the first 1900s, the contents of photographic databases had grown to substantial numbers and methods of classification had become more subtle.

- In modern time, modus operandi Bureau investigatory technique understands that there are variety of important however usually unnoticed ways to link cases aside from direct physical evidences and witness or victim statements.

- These includes :

• **Modus Operandi:** similarities between actions taken by an offender that's necessary for booming completion of crime.

• **Wound Pattern Analysis:** a review of the autopsy or hospital protocols for a victim in a shot to search out similarities between the character and extent of injuries sustained throughout an attack.

• **Victimology:** Similarities or connections between victims.

• **Signature-** Similarities between actions taken by an offender that are unessential for successful completion of crime; actions that recommend a psychological or emotional need.

• **Geographic region or location:** Offenses that have occurred within the same space, or an equivalent form of space.

There is a large quantity of printed data related to the constraints of using MO behavior as the sole basis for linking resolved and unresolved criminal cases, and therefore the importance of understanding the idea of offender signature. However, even the most modern law enforcement case linkage initiatives tend to concentrate on understanding MO behavior alone.

How Modus Operandi Bureau Solves Crime?

There are 3 ways of catching the offender:

- Recognized by an eye-witness.
- Thieves may be catch by the tracing of stolen property.
- By the traces that offender leaves behind whereas committing a criminal offense.

The first two ways are nearly less possible whereas third methodology is far more reliable to analyze by modus operandi bureau to look of crime.

Functions of Modus Operandi Bureau (MOB)

- To study similarities within the modus operandi of criminals and to advise the investigating officers on the basis of the suspect.

- To tell the IOs that unspecified crimes might have been committed by an arrested person.

- To facilitate in establishing the identity of criminal and to furnish reliable information on the antecedents, associates, hide-outs, previous convictions etc. of an arrested person.

- To coordinate to recovered stolen property.

- To disseminates information to keep cops alert and within the lookout for any suspects/missing persons.

- To collect statistical information of crimes, analyze them and spare reviews, testaments, and reports and guarantee that it is regular and periodical.

- To collect numerous kinds of criminals information as well as data.

- To provide information to penal and punitive agencies for their tasks of rehabilitation of criminals, their remand, parole, premature unleash etc.

Chapter 10

▶ **Evidences**

▶ What are Evidences?

▶ Forensic Evidence

▶ Categories of Evidences

▶ Collection and Preservation of Evidences:

What are Evidences?

Evidence is the information which is used in legal proceedings to try to prove the crime or to prove someone innocent. Evidence is obtained anything. For example; documents, objects, or witnesses, etc.

Definition of Evidence under *"Indian Evidence Act, 1872"* Anything by which a disputed matter of fact is proved or disproved. Anything that is clearly evident in court."

Forensic Evidence

Forensic evidence is evidence obtained by scientific methods, Such as; ballistics, blood test, and DNA test which used in court. Forensic evidence helps to establish the guilt or innocence of possible suspects/victim/criminal.

Categories of Evidences

Evidence is divided into numerous categories depending on its characteristics and reliability.

✓ Forensic evidence can be divided into two basic categories:

Physical and **Biological**.

✓ In legal Terms evidence can be divided in two categories:

Direct and **Circumstantial Evidence.**

✓ Other Evidences:

Associative Evidences and **Reconstructive Evidences**

Basic Category

A. Physical Evidence

Physical evidence is any item that can establish whether a crime has been committed or may link the crime and its victim or perpetrator. Anything can be physical evidence that can link the crime scene to the perpetrator.

"In simple words to count physical evidences cannot be possible."

Types of Physical Evidences

1. Body Material:

Body fluids or materials found at a crime scene might include: In case of poison main parts of body, Such as; Liver, Gall bladder, Brain, Kidney, Small intestine, Pancreas, Uterus, Heart and Lungs should be analyzed. Blood, Semen, Saliva and Vomit in dry or liquid state, Hair, Nails, Skeleton, Bone.

2. Botanical Matter:

- Plants
- Fruits
- Seeds
- Leafs
- Wood, etc.

3. Chemical Substance:

- Explosive- any object that has a residue of an explosive is useful.
- Alcohol
- Paint
- Drugs, etc.

4. Weapons:

- Firearms
- Pistol
- Revolver
- Gun
- Bullet
- Cover, etc.

Other arms, such as;

- Knives
- Axe
- Arrow
- Sword
- Hammer
- Scissors
- Stone, etc.

5. Disputed Documents:

Examinations and comparisons conducted by document examiners can be diverse and may involve the following:

- Typewriters, photocopiers, printers, fax machines.
- Handwriting (cursive / printing) and signatures.
- Alterations, additions, erasures, obliterations.
- Indentation detection and/or decipherment.
- Cheque writers, rubber stamps, markers.
- Physical matching.
- Ink, pencil, paper.

6. Petroleum Substance:

Any type of petroleum substance which is likely related to criminal act, Such as; kerosene oil, petrol, etc.

7. Tool Marks:

- Tool mark as any impression, cut, gouge, or abrasion caused by a tool when come into contact with another.

- They consist of small, commonly microscopic, indentations, ridges, and irregularities present on the tool itself. For example, the tip of a screwdriver is never perfectly flat, but shows small ridges along its edge.

8. Impression:

- Finger prints
- Tier marks

- Footprints
- Shoeprints etc.

9. Fibers And Textile:

In Many Cases, Clothes And Rope Are Used In Many Forms.

- Natural fibers
- Artificial fibers
- Threads
- Ropes
- Clothes.

10. Soil:

- Sand
- Clay
- Slit
- Peat
- Loam
- Chalk

Which stick with Tiers, Mudguard, Shoes, Clothes, etc.

11. Glass:

- Pieces of glass , Such as;
- Any Window/ Glass Door

- Glass bottle
- Watch
- Spectacles

12. Objects Of Criminal:

- Identity Card
- Diary

13. Other Evidence:

Any other substances found on the crime scene not mentioned above should be considered in this category.

- For ex- after collision of new building or bridge, sample of debris is physical evidence.
- Things which have numbers. Like; engine, chesis, etc.

Information That Can Be Obtained From Physical Evidence

▸▸ CORPUS DELICTI:

The Latin term corpus delicti refers to the principle that there must be some proof of a crime which has been occurred before a person convicted for that crime.

Corpus delicti literally means **Body Of Crimes**.

▸▸ Identification of suspect:

Fingerprints are valuable evidence to identify and individualize suspect

» Linking suspect with victim:

At the time of crime blood, hair, fiber, etc. can be exchange between suspect and victim which establishes connection.

» Linking of suspect with scene of crime:

Fingerprints, shoeprint or footprint, blood, semen, fiber, hair, tool marks, tier impression, bullet, soil, etc. are evidences which can establish links from suspect to scene of crime.

» Providing investigative leads:

Physical evidences lead police officers in criminal investigation.

» Information about modus operandi:

Criminals, especially habitual criminals have same type of crime manner. Same criminal pattern of behavior helps to caught criminals.

» Verification of statement:

Statement of person (victim, witness, criminal) can be tested after examination and reconstruction of physical evidence.

Nature of Physical Evidence

A. Identification by class characteristics-

Every item has a measurable feature that indicates a restricted group source based on design factors determined prior to manufacture. Physical evidences first identify by its class characteristics.

B. Comparison and individualism-

Marks on an object produced by random imperfections or irregularities on the surfaces of the equipment used to make the object. The personal attribute confirms the object.

Sources of Trace Evidence

At the crime scene, small pieces of physical evidence, such as; Fibers, hair, clothes or carpet can help tell the story of what happened. These are referred to as trace evidence.

Trace evidence can be transferred when two objects touch or when small particles disburse by an action or motion.

For example, paint can be transferred from one car to another in a collision or a hair can be left on a sweater in a physical assault. This evidence can be used to indicate that a person or a thing was present. It can also help in reconstruction of crime-scene.

There are various examples of Trace evidence, Such as; Fibers, hair, soil, wood, gunshot residue, sand, dust and pollen, etc. These are a few examples of trace evidence that may be transferred between people or objects at a time of crime during the commission of crime.

In the early 20th century a famous theory has been given by Dr. Edmund Locard, "Every Contact Leaves Trace". He told the importance of trace evidence in investigation of crime. Investigating officers can develop a link between the suspect and the victim to the crime scene through trace evidence. Since then, trace evidence has been used by forensic experts to solve the crime and rebuild the crime scene.

For Examples;

Clothing

- Clothing is an excellent source of trace evidence.
- Microscopic and macroscopic substances may cling to clothes by static electricity or become caught in the fabric.
- Useful evidence is most likely to be found if the clothes are collected from the suspect or victim after the crime as soon as possible.
- Small items of evidence no bigger than a fiber may easily be dislodged from the clothing and lost.

Footwear

- Shoes and other footwear are valuable items of evidence.
- They may have dust, soil, debris, vegetation, or bloodstains on them.
- In addition to the presence of trace evidence, shoes and other footwear are useful in shoe impression evidence comparison.
- Careful examination of the soil might lead to determination of the path that a suspect took.

Trace Metal Detection

- The trace metal detection test, or TMDT, has been used with mixed results.
- The solution is sprayed on the subject's hands and observed under ultraviolet light. The presence of dark areas indicates the location of metal.
- The TMDT is commonly used to test whether a subject recently held a metal object, Such as; a weapon.

Evidence from the Body

→ Useful trace evidence may be discovered by a careful examination of the suspect and/or victim's body.

→ Hair is sometimes found on the victim's body in rape cases.

→ A close examination of the head, ears, fingernail scrapings, and hands may yield traces of debris from a burglary, assault, or other crime in which there was contact between the subject and another person or the crime scene.

Other Objects as Sources of Trace Evidence

→ Trace evidence may be present on tools and weapons, as well as other objects.

→ Tools used in burglaries may contain traces of building material, metal shavings, paint, and so forth. Similarly, a weapon, Such as; a knife may have hairs or fibers present that may prove to be useful evidence.

→ Larger items may be fruitful sources of trace evidence, for example, a vehicle from a hit-and-run accident.

B. BIOLOGICAL EVIDENCE

Biological evidence refers to samples of biological material.

Types of Biological Evidences-

- Viscera,
- Blood,
- Saliva,
- Bile,
- Stomach Contents,
- Other Tissues (Such As; Liver, Brain, Spleen, Muscle),
- Urine,
- Semen,
- Hair,
- Vitreous,
- Cerebrospinal Fluid, Etc.

Need of the Biological evidence In the Case of:

- Homicide
- Assault
- Rape Or Other Sexual Assaults
- Murder
- Suicide
- Dowry Death
- Accidental Death

- Burglary
- Mass Fatality Incidents
- Motor Vehicle Incidents
- Paternity/Kinship
- Terrorism, Etc.

Divided on the basis of law:

A. Direct Evidence

Evidence in the form of testimony from a witness who actually saw, heard, or touched the subject of questioning.

B. Circumstantial Evidence

It is also known as *Indirect Evidence*.

Circumstantial evidence is evidence which associate with actual evidence at the crime scene.

Other Types of Evidences -

○ Reconstructive Evidence

Reconstructive evidences are those which made by assumption of Investigation Officer, like; what happened at the crime scene.

For example if window Glass of the house is broken, investigation officers will determine that whether glass is broken from inside or outside. Or if gunshot has been fired then shot has been came from which direction.

- **Associative Evidence**

Associative evidence is something that may associate or provide a link to a victim or suspect with a scene or with each other.

Collection and Preservation of Evidences:

Once the discovery done, time of discovery location and appearance of evidence have been thoroughly documented, the evidence must be collected, preserved and, packaged in preparation for submission to the forensic lab.

The following steps should be followed after identification of evidences:

- Evidences should be documented and photographed
- Secure the evidence by placing it in a paper bag/envelope/containers/swabs, etc.
- Seal the bag/envelope/containers/swabs, etc.
- The examiner must note date, and time across the sealed area.
- Examiner must place signature, date, and time on envelope.

Collection and Preservation of Trace Evidence

• Small size evidence should always be double packaged. Double packaging means that the evidence should be first placed into an appropriate container and secured.

- As with all evidence, the investigator or crime scene technician must be concerned with various legal and scientific aspects of collection and preservation of trace materials.

- It is obvious that if evidence needs to be mailed or sent by a parcel carrier, extraordinary care must be taken to preserve fragile substances properly.

- Control or known samples are required in all cases. The investigator should make every attempt to collect a sufficient quantity of known material to be submitted with the items in question.

- The known exemplars must never be packaged with the questioned samples. This separation is necessary to avoid cross contamination of unknown by known specimens.

Keeping the Evidence Secure:

Evidences need to be preserved and secured from the time it is collected. Maintaining Chain of custody is important. The form of chain of custody should contain information about the collected evidence and should always remain with the evidence until it is released to law enforcement. Failure to maintain chain of custody may lead to denial of evidence in court.

Important steps for collecting evidences:

➔ Prevent from Contamination of the sample,

➔ Preserve each specimen separately,

➔ Use and change gloves often,

- ➔ Avoid coughing or sneezing during the collection,
- ➔ Use appropriate tools, Such as; cotton-tipped applicators, sterile water, cardboard swab boxes, separate paper bags, and envelopes.
- ➔ Allow swabs to dry thoroughly,
- ➔ Dry with room temperature,
- ➔ Do not use plastic for evidence collection or preservation.
- ➔ Maintain the individuality of sample by labeling each specimen collected with identifying information.

Chapter 11

▶ **Organizational Structure of Forensic Science**

▶ Category of Forensic Lab

▶ Role of Forensic Science Laboratory

▶ Total Central Labs of Forensic Science in India

▶ Total State Labs of Forensic Science in India

▶ Hierarchy of Lab Administration

▶ Division in Forensic Science Laboratory

Organizational Structure of Forensic Science

There are **38 FSL** operating in the country out of which **31** are under the state government's control. **6** laboratories are managed by the Central government and **1** by CBI.

Category of Forensic Lab

- Central forensic science laboratory
- State Forensic Science Laboratory
- Regional Forensic Science Laboratory
- Local Forensic Science Laboratory

Role of Forensic Science Laboratory

Following functions are performed by Forensic Science Laboratory:

- Producing the evidence in a legally admissible form.
- Examination and analysis of samples/evidences.
- Evaluation and interpretation of result of analysis.
- Assist Investigation officer's and police in:
  - Crime scene investigation and finding evidences.
  - Recognition, collection and preservation of evidences at the crime scene.
  - Analysis, examination and identification of Samples and evidences.
  - Interpretation of evidences in court.

Total Central Labs of Forensic Science in India:

There are total 7 CFSL or Central Forensic Laboratories in India, which are in Hyderabad, Kolkata, Chandigarh, New Delhi, Guwahati, Bhopal and Pune.

Total State Labs of Forensic Science in India:

1. Telangana Forensic Science Laboratory, Andhra Pradesh.
2. State Forensic Science Laboratory, Assam, Guwahati.
3. State Forensic Science Laboratory, Arunachal Pradesh.
4. State Forensic Science Laboratory, Bihar.
5. State Forensic Science Laboratory, Raipur, Chattisgarh.
6. Directorate of Forensic Science, Gandhi Nagar, Gujrat.
7. State Forensic Science Laboratory, Karnal, Haryana.
8. State Forensic Science Laboratory, Junga, Himachal Pradesh.
9. Forensic Science Laboratory, J&K.
10. State Forensic Science Laboratory, Jharkhand, Ranchi.
11. State Forensic Science Laboratory, Bengaluru, Karnataka.
12. Forensic Science Laboratory, Sagar, Madhya Pradesh.
13. State Forensic Science Laboratory, Maharashtra.
14. State Forensic Science Laboratory, Manipur.
15. State Forensic Science Laboratory, Shillong, Meghalaya.

16. Forensic Science Laboratory, Nagaland.
17. Forensic Science Laboratory, Mizoram, Aizawal.
18. State Forensic Science Laboratory, Bhubneshwar ,Orissa.
19. Forensic Science Laboratory, Mohali, Punjab
20. State Forensic Science Laboratory, Thiruvananthapuram, Kerala
21. State Forensic Science Laboratory, Jaipur, Rajasthan
22. Forensic Science Department "Forensic House", Chennai, Tamil Nadu
23. State Forensic Science Laboratory, Tripura, Agartala
24. Forensic Science Laboratory, Lucknow, Uttar Pradesh
25. State Forensic Science Laboratory, Dehradun, Uttrakhand.
26. State Forensic Science Laboratory, Belgachia, Kolkata
27. Forensic Science Laboratory, Port Blair, Andaman and Nicobar
28. Regional Forensic Science Laboratory, Sikkim, Gangtok.
29. Forensic Science Laboratory, Goa.
30. Forensic Science Laboratory, Puducherry.
31. Forensic Science Laboratory, Rohini, Delhi.
32. Forensic Science Laboratory, Andhra Pradesh.

Hierarchy of Lab Administration

A forensic science laboratory is generally headed by Director. The head of division assisted by assistant directors, senior scientific officers, junior scientific officers, senior and junior scientific assistants, laboratory assistants and attendants. The non- technical staff carries out clerical work, maintenance of tools, and other items and other non-scientific duties.

Designation in Forensic Science Laboratory:

- Director
   - Additional Director
      - Deputy Director
         - Assistant Director
            - Senior Scientific Officer
               - Scientific Officer
                  - Senior Scientific Assistant
                     - Scientific Assistant
                        - Lab Assistant
                           - Lab Attendent
                              - Receptionist

Division in Forensic Science Laboratory

Generally Forensic Science Laboratories consist these Divisions:

✓ **Document Division –**

- Identification of handwriting and signatures.

- Detection of forgeries in signatures

- Examination of typewriting and identification of typewriter & Typist.

- Analysis and comparison of different inks and paper.

- Examination and comparison and decipherment of rubber seal impressions on papers or solely.

- Detection of forgeries in travel documents, like passports, traveler cheques, identity cards, credit cards, visas, driving licenses etc.

- Detection and decipherment of secret writings.

✓ **Chemistry Division –**

- Identification of poisons in biological materials such as; viscera, blood, urine, stomach wash, vomit etc.

- Qualitative analysis of narcotics, Psychotropic substances in accordance with the NDPS Act, 1985.

- Analysis and identification of petroleum products and other inflammable substances in arson cases, including dowry deaths.

- Identification of phenolphthalein in trap cases.

- Acids and alkalis analysis and misc. substances examination.

- ✓ **Biology Division –**

  - Identification of various fluids, such as; blood, menstrual blood, semen, saliva, sweat, urine, vomit, fecal matter, nasal discharge, etc. and their stains.

  - Identification and analysation of different parts of animal/human.

  - Identification, origin and comparison of hair. Identification of the actual origin of the hair; i.e., whether the hair is naturally fallen, forcibly removed, hammered, cut or burnt etc.

  - Identification and comparison of all types of fibers, including wool.

  - Determination of origin of person, sex, age, height & identity etc. from skeletal remains, including teeth.

  - Before applying superimposition technique, an anthropological comparison of the human skull with photograph has to be done.

- ✓ **Physics Division –**

  - Examination of glass, paints, different types of metal, coins, keys, etc.

  - Examination and comparison of different types of marks on metals, clothes, paper, leather, glass etc.

  - Examination of telegraph wires.

  - X-ray radiographic examination of packed things. Such as; packets, boxes, letter bombs & other secret contrabands, etc.

  - Deciphering and restoring of erased/altered numbers on automobiles, cycles, machines, typewriters, firearms and tailor marks.

- Testing and comparison of different types of things, such as; sealing waxes, stones, statues, electrical wires, machines, motor parts, electric motors, stoves, refrigerators etc.

- Identification of cause of fire, which is due to electric short-circuiting or otherwise.

- Determination of direction of force on glass, door, window panes, etc. in suicide/murder cases.

- Comparison of different types of materials. Such as; various fabrics, buttons, soil, seals, printing blocks, printing materials, etc.

- Reconstruction of scene of crime.

- Comparison and recognition of recorded voice.

✓ **Serology Division –**

- Forensic serologist has to determine whether the particular weapon related to the incident is stained with human blood or not.

- With the help and results of findings of a serologist, the investigating officer can get a clue in a case which can make case easy to solve and identify the culprit of crime.

- Determination of disputed paternity cases by testing the blood group in question.

✓ **Toxicology Division –**

- Forensic toxicologist determines that which poison is used in particular case.

- In any case, such as; accidental, suicidal or intentional, a toxicologist analyses the viscera and other relevant materials from which it establishes the quality and quantity of poison used.

- With the help of report of a toxicologist, the investigating officer can obtain various clues for detecting the criminals involved.

- Preparation of report according to the judiciary system for further proceedings in the case.

✓ **Ballistics Division –**

- Identification & comparison of firearms and parts of firearms recovered from the scene of crime or the body of the victim, such as; bullets, cartridges, cartridge cases, etc.

- Estimation of the range, direction and angle of firing at the crime scene.

- Examination of air guns and country-made/non-standard firearms for their performance and measurement of their muzzle velocities to check their lethality.

✓ **Explosive Division –**

- Explosives analysis includes explosives (civil, military and IED) and explosive devices used in crime, riots, police firing, encounters etc.

- Re-construction of crime scene where explosion occurred.

- Analysis of explosives and their detection.

- For up-gradation of the working of explosives and explosion residue analysis, this Division is equipped with sophisticated instruments like HPLC System (High Performance Liquid Chromatography).

- Analysis and examination of traces of explosive-residues in post explosion debris to determine the type of explosive involved and how it made.

- Identification of explosives and examination of defused/exploded explosive devices to determine their operation and origin.

✓ **Cyber Forensic Division-**

- Undertakes examination of: Analysis of Mobile phone, memory card, pen drive, hard disk, CD, DVD, and other memory device, Laptop and Desk top computer.

✓ **DNA Typing Division –**

- Undertakes examination of exhibits like:
- Identification of Victim/Perpetrator in violent crimes,
- Disputed Paternity/ Maternity.
- Baby-swapping in neo-natal wards,
- Typing the DNA from different parts and body fluids of human body, such as; Hair, Nail, Tissues, Body fluids and also skeletal remains.

✓ **Polygraph Division (Proposed for establishment) –**

- Polygraph test is exclusively used in criminal investigation in many states including CFSL, CBI New Delhi.
- The results of such test are a useful scientific aid to investigation and being used in interrogation.
- Both psychological and physiological aspects within a person are vital during polygraph test. Though there is no provision in Evidence Act but, the examination results are useful to guide the IOs.

✓ **Photography Division –**

- Photography and videography of scene of crime and crime-related exhibits/objects/evidences from each and every corner and overall view.

- Photography of accused/suspects.

- General & special photography involving ultraviolet, infra-red and visible radiations of all crime exhibits.

- Oblique light, transmitted light/sidelight photography to decipher indented writings/marks.

- Deciphering and identifying of processed photo films in damaged conditions.

- Secret photography involving I.R. and Telephoto-lens techniques.

- Microphotography and macro-photography of documents, numerical, signatures, fingerprints etc.

- Photomicrography of blood, semen, hair, fibers etc.

- Identification of camera and used equipment from the given photo films.

- Secret tape recording of conversation, its origin, alteration, reproduction using special recording device.

- Secret recordings of telephone conversations.

- Preparation of slides, pictures and posters and their projection for audiovisual display.

- Preparation of audio/ video CDs.

✓ **Fingerprint Division –**

- Comparison of fingerprints on documents to identify their identity and relation with criminal.

- Development, lifting and examining of chance prints on exhibits received in the laboratory or at the crime scene to establish the identity of culprit.

- Development of fingerprints on documents, Such as; anonymous letter, threat letter, ransom letter and letter claiming the responsibility for terrorist act by using modern chemical techniques.

- Taking fingerprints of living persons for analysis and examination.

- Comparison and identification of foot prints/footwear prints.

Chapter 12

- **Case Studies**
- Cases on Importance of Forensic report in Indian court
- Cases solved by Forensic Tools

Cases on Importance of Forensic report in Indian court

Ram Narain Vs. State Of Uttar Pradesh

The litigant was sentenced for the offense under section 384 read with section 511 Indian Penal Code. This conviction was specifically founded on the conclusion that two anonymous letters seeking ransom for the kidnapped boy were written by him.
The appealing party completely removed its origin from claiming those letters were delivered in favor of a prosecution case to a handwritten expert, and, accepting the expert declaration, three court below sentenced him to trial.
The only inquiry for consideration in this court was in relation to the legality and appropriateness of the appeal of the party appealing the uncontested testimony of the handwriting expert.
It was urged by the appealing party that it was not safe to record a finding about a person's handwriting only on the basis of the correlation, the handwriting expert's assessment is not conclusive.

M. Nageshwar Rao Vs. State Of Andhra Pradesh

The spouse of the applicant died of cyanide poisoning. Based on the criminological reports, the specialist who prior held the post mortem gave the final opinion on the reason for death and expressed that it was because of cyanide poisoning. Prosecution got blamed that the appellant had mixed up cyanide in a cold drink bottle of Limca and given it to his wife to drink.

Recovered Limca Bottle from residence of appellant supposed to be containing cyanide send to the forensic science laboratory.

Forensic experts expressed that, at the hour of seizure there was no white powder found inside the container as is referenced in the report of the Forensic Science Laboratory. Additionally, the bottle arrived at the Forensic Science Laboratory a lot later and there is no proof about where and with whom the bottle stayed during this period. These situations cast doubt on the appellant.

The realities and conditions of the case may offer ascent to a solid doubt against the litigant yet doubt, howsoever solid, can't happen of evidence. There is no confirmation of the litigant's blame and based on the proof on record it would be very hazardous to hold him blameworthy of homicide and to send him to detainment forever.

Chamkaur Singh Vs Mithu Singh

Sections 45 and 47 of the Act mean that experts, whose opinions are seen on an addressed report, must be sure to be an expert in the relevant field.

The Court needs to take decision keeping in view the evaluation and opinions of experts. Any fault or unskilled behavior because of absence of aptitude by the experts can prompt grave and damages to the parties.

Keeping this in view, this Court has decided that since the assessments of handwriting and fingerprint expert who examine the questioned documents, thumb impressions, signatures, forged documents etc. and so forth is significant and has an immediate bearing on the believability of proof.

Cases solved by Forensic Tools

Murder Mystery of Jane Britton

A girl named Jane Britton found dead of blunt force trauma in her apartment by her boyfriend on 7 January, 1969. Investigators had collected and preserved all evidences from the crime scene. But for many years the case remains unsolved.

After many years preserved DNA from crime scene, matched with a murderer and sexual predator who had been convicted in year of 1973. This case was solved by The DNA testing.

The Lake City Torso Murder

A mutilate body of a young man found behind a gas station in Lake City, Florida. There were many items related to murder was present. In which a mattress cover, waterproof bathtub pad, a shirt covered in blood, and bloody knives were recovered. DNA was preserved from the crime scene. But this matter remained unresolved for many years.

In 2015 after updation of DNA database, preserved DNA of victim got matched with the 16 year old Fred Laster. Police had created a list of suspects after recognizing the victim. At the time of investigation sister of Fred told the police that Ronnie Leon Hyde was the last person who had seen Fred last time and he also had changed his story many times during the investigation of Fred's disappearance.

Ronnie Leon Hyde was a former youth priest and also was a family friend. After getting this information, police take his DNA sample which matched with shirt soaked in blood.

Sarah Clark Case

Police found a dead body of 22 year girl, who was brutally raped and murdered in her apartment on May 16, 1988. Her name was Sarah Clark. Police had collected and preserved all evidences. But this case was remained unsolved for many years.

After updation of DNA databases in June 2001, the Phoenix Police Department's Cold Case Unit brought Sarah Clark's case to the Crime Lab. A DNA profile had been developed from semen taken from Sarah's sexual assault kit. And the recovered male profile had been uploaded to the CODIS databases in 2001.

On January 13, 2005, the unidentified male profile matched with a convicted offender's sample. Offender was identified as 16 year old Mario Pete. He also lived in same building of victim. A bloody palm print found on outside wall of Sarah's apartment was compared to culprit and found to match.

Tiffiny Botello Case

On March 26, 1996, the body of 26-year old Tiffiny Botello was found in an alley. Her body was covered in a black t-shirt. She had injury on her face, neck, and breast area. Postmortem report stated that her death caused by strangulation. Police couldn't solve this case for many years

In April 2003, after examination of the evidence one sperm cell on a vaginal slide was identified and a hair with a root was found on the victim's T-shirt. Those items along with others were forwarded for DNA analysis. A DNA profile was obtained from the samples.

In 2004 profile matched with William Mitchell. In 1996, William Mitchell lived in the area where the victim was last seen and her body found, but was never a suspect in the homicide.

Lonavala Double Murder Case

To catch couple, terrify them by asking them to remove clothes and later to rob them was a Modus Operandi of the two accused who were arrested in the Lonavala double murder case.

On April 3, Sarthak Waghchoure and Shruti Dumbare, two fourth year engineering students of Sinhagad College of Engineering in Lonavala were found murdered near INS Shivaji, near Bhushi dam in Lonavala. They were found naked with their mobiles missing. Vishwas Nangare Patil, Special Inspector General, Kolhapur range, said, "Earlier in two cases, both the accused whom we arrested had robbed two couples in similar manner. They caught them, asked them to remove their clothes and later rob them."

References

* Tewari R K, Ravikumar K V. *"History and development of forensic science in India".* J Postgrad Med [serial online] 2000 [cited 2019 Aug 23]; 46:303. Available from: http://www.jpgmonline.com/text.asp? 2000/46/4/303/250

* Tewari RK. *"Application of Forensic Science in Criminal Justice Administration in the Developing Countries".* The Indian Police Journal1999; XLVI: 78-83.

* Nanda BB, RK Tewari. *"Development of Forensic Science Services at the State Level".* The Indian Police Journal 2000; XLVI-XLVII: 109-119.

* Iyengar NK. *"Growth and Development of Forensic Science in India".* The Indian Police Journal 1961; (Special Centenary Issue):145-151.

* Chatterjee SK. *"History of Fingerprinting in India, The Indian Police Journal (Special Centenary Issue)",* 1961, pp 152-157.

* Tewari RK, AK Ganjoo. *"Fifty years of Forensic Science in India: An Introspection,"* The Indian Police Journal (Special Issue on Indian Police after 50 years of Independence), Vol. XLV, No. 1 & 2, Jan June 1998, pp 105-110.

* http://www.legalserviceindia.com/legal/article-130-the-reliability-of-forensic-sciences.html

* https://www.orangecountynycriminallaw.com/Articles/How-reliable-is-forensic-science.shtml

* https://qrius.com/how-reliable-really-is-forensic-science/

* https://www.dummies.com/education/science/forensics/types-of-evidence-used-in-forensics/

* https://www.slideshare.net/drbhargava5745/introduction-to-forensic-science-labs-in-india

* https://projects.nfstc.org/property_crimes/module02/pro_m02_t04.htm

* https://pressbooks.bccampus.ca/criminalinvestigation/chapter/chapter-8-crime-scene-management/

* https://www.universalclass.com/articles/law/processing-a-crime-scene.htm

* *"Encyclopedia of Forensic Sciences"*, Three-Volume Set, 1-3

* Berg, Stanton O., *"Sherlock Holmes: Father of Scientific Crime Detection," Journal of Criminal Law, Criminology and Police Science* 61, no. 3 (1970): 446–52.

* Cohen, Stanley A., *"The Role of the Forensic Expert in a Criminal Trial," Canadian Society of Forensic Science Journal* 12 (1979): 75.

* Gallop, A. M. C., *"Forensic Science Coming of Age,"* Science & Justice, 43 (2003): 55.

* James, S. H., and Nordby, J. J., eds., Forensic Science— *"An Introduction to Scientific and Investigative Techniques"*, 3rd ed. Boca Raton, Fla.: CRC Press, 2009.

* Kagan, J. D., *"On Being a Good Expert Witness in a Criminal Case,"* Journal of Forensic Sciences 23 (1978): 190.

* Lucas, D. M., *"North of 49—The Development of Forensic Science in Canada,"* Science & Justice, 37 (1997): 47.

* Midkiff, C. R., *"More Mountebanks,"* in R. Saferstein, ed., Forensic Science Handbook, vol. 2, 2nd ed. Upper Saddle River, N.J.: Prentice Hall, 2005.

* National Research Council, *"Strengthening Forensic Science in the United States: A Path Forward"*, Washington, D.C.: The National Academies Press, 2009, http://books.nap edu/openbook.php?record_id=12589&pageR1

* Sapir, Gil I., *"Legal Aspects of Forensic Science,"* in R. Saferstein, ed., Forensic Science Handbook, vol. 1, 2nd ed. Upper Saddle River, N.J.: Prentice Hall, 2002.

* Starrs, James E., *"Mountebanks among Forensic Scientists,"* in R. Saferstein, ed., Forensic Science Handbook, vol. 2, 2nd ed. Upper Saddle River, N.J.: Prentice Hall, 2005.

* Waggoner, Kim. *"The FBI Laboratory: 75 Years of Forensic Science Service,"* Forensic Science Communications, 9, no. 4 (2007).www.fbi.gov/hq/lab/fsc/backissu/oct2007/research /2007_10_research01_test1.htm 000200010270657112

* Saferstein, Richard. *"Criminalistics: An Introduction To Forensic Science"*, Pearson Education, Inc., Upper Saddle River, NJ (2007).

* McClure, David. Report: Focus Group on Scientific and Forensic Evidence in the Courtroom (online), 2007,

* Saks MJ, Koehler JJ. *"The individualization fallacy in Forensic Science Evidence"*. 2008.

* Ram Narain vs State Of Uttar Pradesh

* Chamkaur Singh vs Mithu Singh

* M. Nageshwar Rao V. State Of Andhra Pradesh

* The Indian Penal Code,1860 (Act No. 45 of 1860)

* Prevention of terrorism act, 2002

* Indian evidence act, 1872

* The information technology act, 2008

* The narcotic drugs and psychotropic substances, act, 1985

* Verma S.K. "*Medical Evidence and Court of Law: A Plea for Reforms in India*"; JFMT Vol. 19, No.2, 21-22.

* Kuzmack , N.T.: "*Legal Aspects of Forensic Science*," in R. Saferstein (ed.), Forensic Science Handbook, Englewood Cliffs, N.J.: Prentice Hall, Inc., 1982. Kuzmack, Prentice-

* Kirk, P.L., "*Crime Investigation*", nd ed., New York: John Wiley & Sons, Inc., 1974. 4 2nd

* Chisum , W.J. and Turvey , B.: "*Evidence Dynamics: Locard's Exchange Principle & Crime Reconstruction,*" Journal of Behavioral Profiling, January, 2000, Vol. 1, No. 1. 5 Chisum, Turvey,

****

....

@foreniscfield

www.ingramcontent.com/pod-product-compliance
Lightning Source LLC
Chambersburg PA
CBHW060852220526
45466CB00003B/1336